Longing for Eden Series

THREE PATHS OUT OF PARADISE

Book I

JOHN D. ERICKSON

Cover Design: Alex Tillard

ISBN 978-1719480314

Printed in the United States of America

To Debbie

TABLE OF CONTENTS

FOREWORD

"The purpose in a man's heart is like deep water,
but a man of understanding will draw it out."
Proverbs 20:5

John Erickson is a man of understanding. He has thought
deeply about the complexities of the human heart as well as
about the truth and hope found in Scripture. I've personally
benefited. Having journeyed through the corporate and ac-
ademic world, through many years as a pastor, and now in
leadership at a para-church organization, I've seen a host of
fractured relationships and broken people. Indeed, I am one
of those broken people.

Yet, having known John for over a decade and, more
recently, entering into the insights described in this book,
I have grown to love the discernment with which God has
richly blessed John. John's years in church life and aca-
demia, as a pastor and professor, as an international speaker
and coach for young leaders, as a man who has endured deep
pain as well as profound comfort from the Lord, have given
him a plethora of experiences from which to draw. While
many have written about sin and the Gospel, John leans with

unique insight into how Scripture presents various ways shame and sin affect each of us differently.

Sin and shame come with many disguises. With the Word and Spirit as his instructors, John is a masterful detective. I've witnessed him in person come alongside hurting people. With love and sensitivity, he carefully listens, probes, and (often to their surprise) uncovers painful, deep-seated shame, which he quickly bathes in the healing balm of the Gospel. I've experienced this myself.

John is also a trainer. He's training you, the reader, in this book to lead others to the riches of the Gospel as well. John's insights have influenced how I relate with others. I now have more honest, open, and grace-filled relationships. I feel much more confident in expressing my own vulnerabilities and inviting others to enjoy the freedom of speaking truth intentionally at our shame.

That truth is what I love most about this book. John loves the truth of the Gospel and the Spirit's power to transform people through it. He wants God and God's grace to us in Christ to saturate our lives and flourish within our relationships.

John appreciates the wide range of theological traditions and writes toward a broad audience. If you sense something in his language that differs from your background (as it does mine), there is still the keen perception God has given him for the inner workings of the human heart. As we seek to grow in Christ-likeness, John is offering us a skillfully written gift to encourage us forward in both exploring the anatomy of our sinful hearts as well as experiencing the superabundant love of God for his children.

As you read, may you find deepening joy in the freedom and grace God lavishly offers to those who come needy for Him.

Phil Smith, M.Div.
Executive Director, Leadership Resources International

LONGING FOR EDEN – A JOURNEY

"Why are we reading, if not in hope of beauty laid bare, life heightened and its deepest mystery probed? Can the writer isolate and vivify all in experience that most deeply engages our intellects and our hearts? Can the writer renew our hope for literary forms? Why are we reading if not in hope that the writer will magnify and dramatize our days, will illuminate and inspire us with wisdom, courage, and the possibility of meaningfulness, and will press upon our minds the deepest mysteries, so that we may feel again their majesty and power? What do we ever know that is higher than that power which, from time to time, seizes our lives, and reveals us startlingly to ourselves as creatures set down here bewildered? Why does death so catch us by surprise, and why love? We still and always want waking."
Annie Dillard

Longing. Even when you are unaware, it moves you. In life's most poignant moments, it draws you deeper: realizing how much you love someone, packing your little sister's U-Haul, being skin-to-skin with your freshly born daughter, loading your son's military gear into the trunk of his car, gently placing a rose on top of a lifelong friend's casket. Longing tugs on your heart when you are exhilarated in joy or devastated in grief—powerful, deep, buried within you—

searching for intimate contact, safe space, clarity, meaning. Longing is woven into your very existence as a human, pulling you toward something ultimate, somewhere beyond.

Eden. A place of perfection. Order overcoming chaos, infinite creativity at the largest and smallest scale fully expressing life, vitality, growth. Relationships flowing from love, void of shame. Life procreating life with joy that knows no pain or death. Caretaking beauty for pleasure and productivity, without toil or hardship. Satisfying activity with purpose and meaning. Complete peace with no hint or desire for violence. The ability to enjoy and reflect the creation. All need for sustenance, intimacy, community sated. A place to be human in all the ways we were designed: naked, unafraid, flourishing with vulnerability and trust.

From the moment we screamed out our first breath, we have been longing for Eden. For millennia, the sentient beings and inanimate aspects of our world have been groaning for the recovery of that perfect order. If there is any way for this life to be bearable, even joyful, it is in the hope of recovering what we had in Eden.

As we pore over the storyline God provides us in Scripture, we learn that hope is not futile. As soon as the angel's flaming sword banished us from the Garden of Eden, our

Father committed himself to recover what was lost. His persistence is powerful and mysterious as he moves and shapes that story to bring us to a perfect, restored creation. No amount of evil, chaos, pain, or death thwarts his perseverance. He made the ultimate sacrifice of his son to ensure the possibility of full redemption, for his children and all of his creation.

As we pore over the storyline God provides us in Scripture, we learn that hope is not futile.

Longing for Eden has been a persistent motivation in my own life, and for the last twenty-five years, I have been intimately involved with walking others into their own fulfillment of that longing. My passion has developed into a deep desire to show God's children, especially those he has gifted with leadership abilities, how their hearts work, and how to flow freely in all the talent and anointing he has poured into them. As God restores what was lost in the first Eden, he is revealing his redemptive purpose to each of our hearts. He is showing us the specific and irreplaceable ways we fit into his body and build his kingdom back into that perfect Edenic reality. My own purpose has become clearer as I walk with emerging adults, mentoring and coaching them toward their own specific roles in God's story.

I have been accompanied on this journey by my friend and colleague, Dennis Humphrey, who is a practicing counselor. In observing hundreds of hearts and lives we have noticed a set of lacunae that are consistently thwarting people from fulfilling God's purposes. There is a gap in understanding of how their hearts work, especially why they respond to emotional pain the way they do. There is a fundamental lack of skill in listening to the Holy Spirit, in their reading of Scripture, and in their relationships. There is a pervasive resistance to finding and developing mentoring relationships as a way to provide and receive wisdom. We are certainly not the first to notice these challenges to building leaders for the kingdom; books, seminars, conferences, podcasts, and YouTube videos abound on every issue we will address. At the same time, we sense there is a unique and necessary contribution to make, especially in the circles where we have developed personal relationships. Likewise, those who have heard and implemented our perspectives have encouraged us to document them for a wider audience.

In this series of books, Dennis and I will address several areas of leadership development: our longings, our conflicts, how we find fulfillment, and how we walk with others in their longings. This first book will describe a paradigm to understand our hearts more clearly, allowing the Spirit more freedom to make Jesus obvious in us and enable us to develop relationships that flourish. The second book will provide a way to navigate through the chaos of our relational conflicts. The third book will address the fundamentals of becoming a holistic leader, discovering purpose, overcoming the power of shame, and listening to the Spirit as a way of life. The fourth book will present mentoring as a necessary way to walk with others in their longings and call current leaders to fill the gap for the next generation of leaders in the Kingdom.

We write from the perspective of western Christians who have a relationship with God through his son, Jesus. At the same time, the ideas in these books, rooted in our understanding of Scripture, have application to every human being. Wherever you are in your development or acceptance of spiritual life, knowing how your heart works is invaluable for your relationships and endeavors. We have used these tools and perspectives in numerous settings with people from all walks of life, and they have translated effectively. We encourage you to apply them to your relationships as well.

We also write with a desire for all the various streams of Christian faith to engage this fundamental paradigm without being distracted by our particular background. For example, throughout this book we use the idea of listening to the Spirit as an important skill for understanding how to apply the concepts we describe. This language is not meant to polarize. We use it deliberately to draw in the biblical gift and necessity to live our lives from our intimate relationship with God, which is provided to us in and through his Spirit. From the prophecies of Jeremiah and Ezekiel, the witness of the forerunner John the Baptist, the teaching of Jesus in John's Gospel, the descriptions of the early church in Acts, Paul's letters to the early church, and Jesus' Revelation to John, we are taught to observe, listen, hear, submit, walk with, live in, receive from, pray, and worship through God's Spirit. He enlivens and applies the Word he spoke into and from the biblical writers to us in our present moments, and he brings us the constant encouragement and power of God's presence. The necessary sign of one who has believed the Gospel of Jesus is the internal reality of God's Spirit. The demonstration of God's character in our lives is the fruit of his Spirit.

The fulfillment of our longing for Eden is guaranteed by the down payment of the Spirit in us. In his letter to the Galatian church, Paul summarizes our path out of root sins: "If we live by the Spirit, let us also keep in step with the Spirit. Let us not become conceited, provoking one another, envying one another." Thus we summarize walking, living, keeping in step with the Spirit with the lifestyle of Jesus, who listened to his Father and did what his Father was doing.

The biblical description of Eden enlightens our imaginations with stunning beauty and inexhaustible sustenance. One aspect of that paradise makes our hearts pang even more than the abundance and atmosphere. Father God made it his habit to walk there among the trees, speaking freely and communing closely with his first children. Presence. We long for his presence with us, unencumbered by sin or shame. We know it is coming. The last few pages of God's story show us a vision of his presence among us again. We also know he has started walking with us; we can bring others along. Longing for Eden will one day become Living in Eden.

1

FROM TOLERATED TO TREASURED

"A carefully cultivated heart will, assisted by the grace of God, foresee, forestall, or transform most of the painful situations before which others stand like helpless children saying 'Why?'"
Dallas Willard

Your life and your relationships will either flourish or flounder based on how well you know your own heart. Learning how your heart works is a lifelong process with ongoing, meaningful steps in every moment you walk with the Father, exploring the riches of his grace. The process is intensely personal, and yet it flows out of our experiences with people around us—personal, not private. As I walk with young people who are discovering how to listen to the Spirit and to their hearts, it is often in our shared experiences that we understand more clearly what is happening and how to express it in ways that bring others along. For a number of years, Dennis and I have been developing and sharing a paradigm for understanding our hearts, especially our longings, and how they drive us to respond to pain the way we do. We use this method to help groups and people understand their experiences, and in almost every situation, they discover valuable insight into themselves and their relationships. The most effective way to describe this is to interweave some of my own personal narrative, and the narratives of others we have walked alongside. As you experience these journeys, you will find yourself joining our stories with your own, and in that you too will develop fresh insight into your own heart.

Your life and your relationships will either
flourish or flounder based on how well
you know your own heart.

So, some of my story. I was adopted when I was about eighteen months old by a couple in their early thirties. My adopted mother was the daughter of Croatian immigrants; she knew she would never have children of her own because of a previous illness. My adopted father was also adopted, given away to an older Swedish couple during the depression by a family who could not afford to feed him. My Croatian and Swedish grandparents did make for entertaining family gatherings. I do not know much about my biological parents, other than I was an unexpected pregnancy from two college students. I have never pursued knowing more about them. Jerry and Millie Erickson loved me and my adopted sister as they would their own children. I always felt cared for and safe in my adopted home. I knew I was expected to behave well, work hard in school, treat others properly, go to church, not take drugs, go to college, marry a nice girl, provide grandchildren, and call my mother.

My adopted family was not especially adept at expressing positive emotions, affirmation, or physical affection, but I never felt abused, save for the ever-present threat to go dig the dandelions from our expansive backyard. Much later in life, I noticed something that other adopted children express: a haunting sense of abandonment in my heart, an orphan spirit of sorts. This sense of abandonment in others has been documented professionally, but I did not pay much attention until I realized one of its more profound effects in myself. There has always been a nagging dissatisfaction in all my relationships, something thwarting my ability to feel intimacy. As I thought back over my life, I remembered from a young age that the best I could ever feel, the most confidence I could ever have in a relationship, was to be tolerated. I walked into every relationship, every classroom, every office, every meeting, every friendship, every church, every job, my marriage, raising my children, even coming before my Father God, knowing in the deepest part of my heart that no matter what I said or did, I would smack up against the ceiling of tolerance. I almost never felt the confidence of being liked by someone. My mind knew that people loved me and that God loved me, but I had no heart experience of this. I was like a color-blind person who could assign color names to various shades of brown or grey because others told me what they were.

I know now that I longed for respect and the feeling of worth and intimacy, ultimately the sense of being wanted, not abandoned. Always feeling tolerated trained my heart to abandon the effort of expecting affection or intimacy from people. I learned to guard my heart, to push away attempts to know me deeply, to pursue success and adventure with my skills, to keep people at a distance by always being smart, capable, and mostly, by being right. Looking back, I can see my Father was pursuing my heart all along; he continually put people and situations in my life to lead me beyond the mindset of tolerance. Two circumstances broke through the wall I had built around my heart.

After being at seminary through two master's degrees and a doctorate, teaching seminary classes for over a decade, pastoring a church for twelve years, leading a city-wide prayer movement, speaking and teaching internationally, I was asked to move to another city and become the senior pastor at another church. With some reluctance, but having the unanimous support of the church members and the board, I accepted the position. Four months later, the same board slid a letter across the table essentially paying me to leave immediately. I was not the leader they were expecting or wanting, and they would like me to go quietly. I did leave, and it was one of the most shameful, painful feelings of failure I have ever known. All my training, skills, and experience hit a brick wall. I lost my motivation and desire to pursue any kind of ministry, and entered a decade of staring into a black hole. But through it, the Lord continued to chip away at my heart wall.

Almost twelve years after leaving pastoral ministry, attempting to get my footing in leadership development, I went to San Francisco to visit a couple of younger guys I had been mentoring. One of the evenings we went up to the roof of the building where we were staying. As we were enjoying the glow of the city, car lights climbing the steep hills, and the Golden Gate Bridge reflecting into the bay, I began to describe my heart to one of them. After years of recovering from that break up, my heart was more open and softer, but I was still living from a place of abandonment and tolerance. Again, I knew in my head that God and people loved me, but my heart felt empty.

As I succumbed again to numbness, my friend's compassion and determination were coming to a boil; with surprising suddenness he stood up, marched over to me, plunked down on my lap, and wrapped his arms around me. For an awkward moment I wondered what anyone observing would think of two guys snuggling on a rooftop. He spoke into my ear the heart of the Father for me: he does not in any way tolerate me, he loves me with the deepest affection possible, and I do not need to believe ever again that I am abandoned. Then my friend sat up and put his hands on the sides of my face, like a small child whose attention he needed, and forced me to look straight into his eyes. He told me that the Father wanted to look into me and express his love for me, and I could not turn away. This young man, half my age, became the conduit of the Father's heart into mine.

Something profound happened to me that night, the most heart changing event since the night almost forty years ago when I gave my heart to Jesus. After my friend moved from my lap, I watched the metal gate and bars that guarded my heart for so many years fall off; my raw heart was exposed for the first time. I also sensed the presence of the Father next to me, touching my chest with his fingers, sending jolts of electric love into my being. He was telling me that this is what his love feels like, and it will always be there. This was the first time that I *experienced* what his love feels like. It was like I was born again, again. My friend gave me glasses that allowed my color-blind heart to see the true colors of love for the first time. I saw and experienced being treasured by my Father.

From that night on a rooftop in San Francisco, I have not had a glimmer of only being tolerated. I am free. I walk into meetings with pastors, leaders, students, family, friends, my wife, with no need to hide my heart, no sense that I will be tolerated. I know, and I mean I know in my heart, that I am loved. I can choose to spend my spiritual and emotional energy listening to the Spirit and loving the people around me. One of the reasons I was ready for my friend to grab me was because I had learned more about my heart, and what it was really longing for.

Those two events, being abruptly removed from ministry and experiencing the Father's love in a new way, were the circumstances through which I discovered how my heart works. Of course, these events were not isolated from my nearly four decades of walking with God, reading, studying, preaching, teaching, hearing, worshiping, and praying through his Word. The heart experience I had of the Father's love was possible because of the work of the Spirit through his Word over many years.

One instance of hearing his Word ignited a spark in my heart for developing the paradigm in this book. A seminary chapel preacher highlighted the story of the ruined loincloth from Jeremiah 13, pointing out that the broken relationship Israel had with God was due to three fundamental issues, root sins he labeled them: pride, idolatry, and unbelief. The idea of three root sins being the cause of all human failure was seminal for my understanding of the human heart. I continued to look through Scripture for other evidence. It turns out that these three root sins come into play from the beginning of God's story; they are the very issues Eve faces as she listens to the serpent and makes her fateful choice. These three root sins rise over and over again in the history of Israel, the Psalms and Proverbs, the pleadings of the prophets, the issues facing the early church. Even the temptations Satan brought to Jesus at the beginning of his ministry were specifically pride, idolatry, and unbelief. I will unpack some of these biblical passages in interludes between the chapters as we proceed.

Each person I have worked with consistently exhibits an entitlement to a specific longing in his or her heart.

As I began to compare the biblical storyline to the stories of young people I was teaching and mentoring, I noticed that each one of them reacted to their life and related to others from the perspective of one particular root sin. Certainly there is overlap among the three, and we all exhibit pride, idolatry and unbelief in various ways. Yet, each person I have worked with consistently exhibits an entitlement to a specific longing in his or her heart. Those who react from pride are ultimately driven by their need for respect. Idolatry is rooted in a deep desire to be valued. Unbelief is characterized by a fear of being abandoned and unloved. I have presented this idea to audiences in churches, businesses, classrooms, and counseling sessions and with dozens of people I have mentored and coached across cultures from the U.S., Eastern and Western Europe, Africa, Asia, the Middle East, and Central and South America. I am convinced that how we respond to pain or to our need for intimacy reflects something deeply seated in our hearts: a root sin that motivates us, a distinct language and behavior that creates our words and actions. This root sin is the primary focus of where God's Spirit wants to change your heart.

The following chapters will focus on each root sin in turn, describing how it develops and shapes our responses and how the Spirit wants to redeem it for his purposes. Chapter Five will describe how the three root motivations interact with each other, and how to relate well to those from each group. The intention here is not to blindly categorize people into simple groups and then predict or judge their behavior accordingly. Nor is this paradigm meant to compete with or replace other valuable emotional and personality assessment tools. Our desire is to understand how our hearts are inclined, and to learn how the Spirit wants to move us toward each other and toward the Father. As you find yourself resonating with one or more descriptions, ask the Spirit how he wants you to respond or what he wants to show you about yourself or your relationships. You will also find inspiration and encouragement from the stories and exhortations in Scripture, especially as you learn how Jesus acts and responds to the various situations in his world.

Recently, I watched a YouTube video of an older color-blind man receive what he thought was a pair of sunglasses for his birthday. When he tried them on he stood almost paralyzed as he saw colors he had never before seen in his life, a type of eyesight that had only been described to him, but he had never experienced himself. He started to weep almost uncontrollably, and then he walked around his yard looking at flowers, plants, signs, cars, people. Everything was the same, yet it was all brand new. Understanding how your heart works is like that. Everything and everyone are still there; yet you can see yourself, and everyone else, with God's eyes. It is exhilarating. Enjoy.

INTERLUDE
CREATION – THE SOURCE OF PURPOSE

"An honest observer must admit that the world we occupy makes a powerful statement about its origin and purpose. Upon the vastness of space beyond us, over the grandeur of the geography around us, and within the beauty, variety, and complexity of life itself, there is the obvious signature of a creative genius. Furthermore, the one who ponders in faith will see the hand of God—the Creator who spoke out of his being to form everything that exists. Thus, the Hebrew Scriptures open, without apology or defense, to describe the work of a Creator God whose very words turned nothing into something: darkness into light, void into stars and planets, chaos into water and earth, dust into life. This was a serious and powerful claim for its original readers."

Siniša Hamp

You are a created being. When this profound revelation becomes truth at the core of your being, it has the power to set the course of your life for eternity. It is a revelation because it does require faith to accept and comprehend. This truth resonates in a deep place because faith leads you to recognize and turn toward ultimate value in your heart. There is a built-in core of Imago Dei that resonates with God's voice of revelation to you. You are able to access that place in your heart through worship: recognizing and turning toward the surpassing value of God.

You are a created being. Ponder the implications of that truth. You are neither a product of chance, nor a consequence of your own thought or power. Something outside of you made your existence possible, and from the evidence of the complexity of your being, a creative genius far beyond yours is responsible. Besides the evident marvel of your physical form and life, there is your ability to think, decide, emote, relate, survive; beyond those realities is your inner, more subtle knowledge of the transcendent. You have a soul, an ability to connect to something at the deepest part of your being, something spiritual that reaches out to the initiator of you.

Being created means that not only does your existence have purpose, but that purpose is intricately tied to the one who created you. In fact, as a created being, you belong to your creator, and he sets that purpose himself. From what he has revealed about himself in Scripture, that purpose will always commingle two aspects: what will expose most clearly his being and character, and what will be the absolute best for you. He ensures those by creating you in his image. He built his heart, character, and purpose into the fabric of your being. You are tuned to resonate and echo at the frequency of the one who fashioned you, and your deepest longings and sense of fulfillment will always be a function of your alignment with him.

Not only does your existence have purpose, but that purpose is tied to the one who created you.

Being created means that everyone around you also has the same longings and potential. Your creator is relational by nature; God the Father, his Son, and their Spirit live in perfect unity, and that too has been built into your existence. You have an innate desire to be in relationships that are safe places to live out your purposes together. Your ability to move with people in these relationships depends on your knowledge of your creator and of what he has created in you. Your ability be led and to lead others toward their created purposes is a product of knowing God's heart and your own heart.

Being created means that you are not the center of the

universe, your own nor anyone else's. The center of the universe, yours and everyone's, is your creator. Life, relationships, work, learning, discovering, caring, worshipping only have meaning when they center on God and flow from his being. Thinking about yourself, your relationships, your life situation from a God-centered perspective is the only way to move and flow in your created purpose.

Being created means that you have the capacity to live from the life of God in you, to fulfill his purpose for your life. He is always working to redeem his creation through you. God is transforming self-promoting knowledge and ability into spiritual wisdom that radiates his truth. He is turning self-focused idolatry to an inspiration that amplifies another's value and gifts. He is overcoming people-pleasing unbelief and fear with faith that brings his true peace over hearts and lives.

At the same time, God's desire to redeem his creation implies that something is wrong. Scripture also reveals that the created order has been thwarted, and you are in the process of being redeemed. That process involves overcoming aspects of your human nature that were built into you. What you will discover as we proceed is that you have a set of ingrained entitlements that are the source of most of your responses to people and the world around you. These involve the need for respect, value, and love. One of these plays a strong role in your own life; a subtle but profound sense of competition, deception, manipulation, or control often provides your first response to pain.

Your lifelong challenge is to overcome the power and effect of these root distortions of your created purpose: pride, idolatry, unbelief. A pride-based person becomes humble before Christ and receives his wisdom, an idolatry-based heart submits to Christ and recognizes its ability inspire others to the fullest potential of their gifts in the Spirit, an unbelief-driven person releases paralyzing fear to Christ and becomes a channel of his peace.

How do you move toward living out your created purpose? Overcoming your independence and personal identity formation means acting in the moment with two focuses: opening space in the moment for the Spirit to highlight God's value of the person or event, and seeing God's larger purpose for their life or for that moment and encouraging movement in that direction. In other words, reacting out of love and focusing on the value and purpose of others.

2

FROM RESPECT TO WISDOM

*"Let your old age be childlike, and your childhood like old age;
that is, so that neither may your wisdom be with pride, nor your
humility without wisdom."*
Augustine of Hippo

Do you ever speak to someone important in your life,
a close friend, parent, or child, and get a very different response than you expected? Allow my friend's twenty-one-
year-old daughter to explain. She was on a missions trip to
Central America at the time.

*There's a couple of girls that I like here because
they're real, funny, and sincere. One of them told
me that I'm so put together and that I reminded her
of Katniss, the hero girl from The Hunger Games
books. That's actually a huge compliment haha :).
I'd like to be as fierce and confident and courageous
as everyone seems to think, but I'm really not. Some-*

times I can be a huge ball of anxiety and stress and anger and sadness, which you guys know quite well.

That is a conflict we feel all the time: we would like to respond from strength, confidence, grace, from who we want to be, but our emotions seem to push us to respond from inadequacy, shame, or fear. For example, I am going along fine, play a couple of games of racquetball with one of the college guys I mentor, get beaten, and feel like a failure because my respect button got pushed. I feel incompetent because I'm not good enough, again. I'm no longer interested in encouraging him. Or, Debbie and I are having a nice conversation over dinner until I mention a trip I am planning to Eastern Europe, suddenly she stiffens, her tone changes. "I hate it when you're gone; you travel too much. Weren't you just there?" Her comfort button got pushed. She feels pain and fear. Recovery will probably go into the next day. Or, your teenage son's face falls as you discuss his plans for the summer, he turns to walk away: "you aren't hearing me, you don't understand me, my ideas aren't important to you." His value button got pushed. He feels worthless. In each of these cases, relationship and intimacy were suddenly truncated because of a powerful heart reaction. Typically, we would simply blame our responses to each other on fatigue, immaturity, or selfishness in the moment, and we would ignore the deeper, more ingrained causes. Your sense of shame would quickly tell you something degrading about yourself and your inability to be in an effective relationship, you would absorb your failure to connect, and you would change the subject. Rather than flourish, your relationship would continue to flounder, at least in that area. What if there was a way to understand why we respond the way we do, and in knowing, have the ability to move through the pain into reconnection? What if we could hear a different story than shame's lies? Our Father wants us to flourish in our life and relationships, just like in Eden. Come explore a way toward that place.

Which scenario is more painful for you? What do you avoid more avidly?

To feel like a failure, incompetent, ultimately: *disrespected?*

To feel worthless, unheard, misunderstood, ultimately: *devalued?*

To feel unloved, uncared for, insecure, ultimately: *disliked?*

This question of what hurts more helps to focus on the basic longing in your heart. All three of these needs interplay in your heart at times, but one of them most likely drives your primary reaction to unexpected resistance or pain. It is not necessary at this point for you to come to a definitive decision. As we describe each root need, and how it moves us in our responses, you will find yourself resonating with various aspects of each motivator. Allow them to settle, and ask the Spirit to bring his word and truth over your mind and heart.

My own response as a pride-based person may help. I hate failure. Not so much the failure of others, or of the world around me, although those can be heartbreaking. What I really hate is my own sense of failure, and I have been aware of that from the time I can remember my first thoughts. Whether it was learning to play my first toy organ and then the violin, learning long division, spending less time in the principal's office than in class, avoiding a backyard session of dandelion pulling as punishment for some mother-displeasing infraction, figuring out how to walk in a coordinated-enough way not to knock down the Christmas tree in the middle of my grade school with my violin case (again), catching more baseballs with my hands than my face, coming in somewhere other than last at any of my high school swim meets, having a conversation with a given teacher, girl, or classmate that did not permanently end the relationship, not pursuing my life-long dream of being a physician, or making it more than four months in a pastoral position without being asked to leave, I have grown to loathe failure more than just about anything else in my life.

That is not to say that I have been a failure at everything. I have been quite successful at a few things. But in the process, I have learned how much my hatred of failure has driven my responses and decisions and how entitled I have felt to success, at the cost of relationships and other meaningful accomplishments. Three decades of pastoring, teaching, counseling, mentoring, and coaching people in numerous places and cultures, has shown me that I am not in any way alone in my hatred of failure. I have observed that success and failure are only parts of a larger and deeper desire for respect, which drives several other realities for those of us with this proclivity. My need for respect pushes me in several directions. Not only do I need to be successful, but in order to be successful, I need a lot of clarity about what is going on and why it is happening. I will push people until I get the clarity I need to make sure I am right, because being right means I am competent and successful, and being successful means I will get the respect I so desperately need to justify my sense of personal worth.

All of these—being right, competence, success, clarity, ultimately respect, when they are used in a self-focused way—are the manifestations of the root sin of pride. I have used my arrogance in these various ways to protect my heart from the voice of the orphan, from the pervasive sense of tolerance. Anytime anyone got too close, I could push them back on their heels to a safe distance. Pride could give me a hit of self-confidence that lasted long enough to bully my way through the tolerance, and feel important, competent, and okay, even if just for a moment. The addiction to respect led me to a powerful sense of entitlement. If I got a whiff of disrespect from someone, there was very little chance I would make an effort to connect with them.

If I do not submit to the Word and the Spirit for long enough, my entitlement will harm or even end my ability to be in intimate relationship.

For pride-based people, a conversation or meeting often follows this path: It hurts to feel like a failure. I want to be right. I need to be respected. I demand clarity and push for competence. I become competitive so I can grab whatever respect is possible. I'm not really concerned in the moment how much pain or discomfort I might cause or how unvalued the other person might feel; I just need to get my fix of respect. All of this can be invisible or seem innocuous to the outside observer, especially if I have some awareness of relationship dynamics or decent communication skills that allow me to hide my motives. Over time, if I do not submit to the Word and the Spirit for long enough, my entitlement will harm or even end my ability to be in intimate relationships.

Through the decade after leaving pastoral ministry, the Lord showed me how much the root sin of pride had infiltrated my heart and my relationships. He revealed to me how many of my friends, colleagues, and family members I had alienated or harmed. Ultimately, he showed me that I am not entitled to respect nor to being right, competent, or successful. These are not improper things to pursue in the right circumstances, but when I demand them as an independent path to significance, they are toxic.

The antidote to pride came as I reflected on what it means to have the Spirit of God present in my life. Being filled with the Spirit is the same gift that Jesus had as a man on earth. Jesus listened to the Spirit as he acted and spoke exactly as the Father. Jesus derived his identity and significance from the words of the Father, "you are my beloved Son, in you I am well pleased." When we submit our hearts to Jesus, the very same gifts become ours: we receive the Holy Spirit, and we come into the family of God as his sons or daughters, in whom God is well pleased. The presence of the Spirit in my heart gives me the ability to submit to his Word, to come to a place of humility before God, to become a channel of his love and truth into the lives of others. Being right about truth, competent to communicate it clearly, and successful at building bridges into others' hearts are the ways the Spirit redeems my pride-based responses. The Spirit redeems pride by taking it through the path of humility to wisdom. He turns my heart away from applying truth, clarity, competence, and success in order to gain respect. Instead, I can apply that truth from the Spirit into another's life. He provides insight into the truth and the heart of another so I can be a source of his wisdom. Wisdom is the antidote to the root sin of pride.

If your heart resonates with this description of the pride root sin, begin to look over your relationships and allow the Spirit to show you how it shows up. Each of the root sins looks and sounds a bit different in every person; you will express your entitlement with a particular dialect and emphasis based on your personality and experiences.

The Spirit redeems pride by taking it through the path of humility to wisdom.

I know a couple who both are pride-based, for example, and although they both love to be right, competent, successful, and respected, those entitlements manifest in very different ways. The woman is outspoken about her opinions, takes charge, demands clarity vocally, and falls hard when she fails at something. The man is far subtler in his outward expression of competence and success, holding back his opinions and perspectives until the others in the conversation have had their say. Once he has calculated the abilities and weaknesses of everyone, he then asserts himself to prove his superiority. This couple has learned how root sins play out in their relationships, and they can now speak respect and wisdom into each other's lives. You also can learn to be aware of your own responses to feeling incompetent, disrespected, or like a failure. The Spirit can teach you to drop your entitlements and listen for what another person needs. You will learn to speak wisdom through your personality that encourages others to submit to the Word and the Spirit themselves.

PRIDE

I feel like a failure

I want to be right

I need to be respected

I demand clarity and push for competence

I am competitive

But...

I am not entitled to respect

I am filled with the Spirit

He brings me to humility

He gives me his insight

So...

I am a channel of God's wisdom

WISDOM

INTERLUDE
JEREMIAH 13 – THE LOINCLOTH

"I'm just not sure that I want to trust God with my life and my future." I looked over my coffee cup across a small table toward a young man in his early twenties. His misty eyes betrayed deep shame, anger, disappointment, confusion, and longing. A talented musician with skills in writing, music, and media, recently married to a beautiful, creatively gifted young woman, he was home from a distant state visiting family for the holidays. A few months prior to our meeting that morning, he had pursued a dream to tell his stories using short films. His new wife agreed to leave her established and promising position, as well as the family and community where she had grown up. After some months of fundraising and planning, they moved a thousand miles away for him to work in a media production group. Almost nothing had gone as he hoped. Their finances were half what they needed. She could not find a position in her field. The production team and role were not what he had envisioned. They were alone and unconnected to any sort of community there. His funding situation, as well as wife's feeling insecure and unsafe in their living circumstances, made it seem like he needed to abandon his dream in that place and return home. He felt abandoned by God, like a failure to his wife, without any direction or purpose. After listening to his story, I sensed that God was using this situation to raise his attention; his Father was asking my friend simply to trust him. That was the very thing he was not willing to do. His entitlement to independence was just too powerful. He had to figure it out for himself. He felt that was the only way to restore some measure of his dignity. The longing call of God for his heart was a faint, unheeded whisper.

So it was for God's people when God called the prophet Jeremiah to speak over their lives in the face of impending national catastrophe. For decades, even centuries, they had sought to assuage their need for security and guidance from every source but their Father God. What is most poignant about this story in Jeremiah is how heartfelt God's longing is for his people. God had a vision for his beloved Israel. He had created them as his own, a people that carried his very name, meant to receive who he is and reflect that to the world around them. He wanted to be in an intimate relationship with them. He saw them as his prized children with a unique identity, as an object of delight, as a showcase of his love and grace. In their pride and rebellion, Israel wanted nothing to do with God's vision for them. They did not trust him, and they preferred, even demanded, to worship anything but him. This is the recurring pattern of Israel's history. It is the theme of the old testament prophets, and it is the story of Jeremiah in particular.

Along that story, God directs Jeremiah into a living parable. Go buy some new underpants; wear them around for a while. Now, take off your underpants and bury them under a rock in a riverbank. Sometime later, go back and dig up your underpants and see what you find. Of course, they are spoiled: moldy, rotted fabric, bug-eaten holes, good for nothing, utterly useless for their intended purpose. They have now become a powerful symbol. Why underwear? They cover, cling to, and protect the most intimate, the most shame oriented, parts of one's body. God desired to have his people cling intimately to him, to cover their shame with his love and grace, to care attentively for them. That ruined loincloth was a picture of what had happened to Israel's relationship with God and what God was doing in response. He does not mince words to declare why their relationship was broken: "I will spoil the pride of Judah, and the great pride of Jerusalem. This evil people, who refuse to hear my words, who stubbornly follow their own heart and have gone after other gods to serve them and worship them." Israel was living out her root sins: an entrenched pride that made God irrelevant in their national and personal lives, an inexplicable unbelief that refused to trust God at his word, a rampant desire to revere pagan idols rather than their Creator. For them to come back into a relationship with him, God had to take a painful path with them; in order to restore their hearts, he had to break their hearts. Ultimately, after decades of prophetic warnings, Israel watched the Babylonian army devastate their beloved Jerusalem, and take them on a long march into exile.

God's desire has always been to keep his children moving toward the redemption he promised.

God's desire has always been to keep his children moving toward the redemption he promised Adam and Eve in the garden, and every generation since then. The first couple had attempted to hide their nakedness and sin-induced shame under a loincloth of fig leaves. Deeply injured and saddened by their lack of trust, only the Father's compassion and mercy could overcome their failure with a view to save their race ultimately. The new animal skin loincloths he fashioned for them foreshadowed a long process of sacrifice to keep that promise.

God did not abandon his people to languish in Babylon permanently. His word maintained; even before their nation was destroyed, he was laying the foundation of a new relationship with them. "But this is the covenant that I will make with the house of Israel after those days, declares the Lord: I will put my law within them, and I will write it on their hearts. And I will be their God, and they shall be my people. And no longer shall each one teach his neighbor and each his brother, saying, 'Know the LORD,' for they shall all know me, declares the LORD" (Jer 31:33-34 ESV).

The New Testament prophet, John, saw the powerful fulfillment of God's ultimate plan, which he recorded in Jesus' Revelation to him. In the seventh chapter, he describes the pulsating din of worship before God's throne: "After this I looked, and behold, a great multitude that no one could number, from every nation, from all tribes and peoples and languages, standing before the throne and before the Lamb, clothed in white robes, with palm branches in their hands, and crying out with a loud voice, 'Salvation belongs to our God who sits on the throne, and to the Lamb!'" The shame-covering loincloths have been replaced with clean white robes made pure by the sacrificial blood of Jesus, the Lamb of God, who died shamefully naked. Their purpose, our purpose, has been fulfilled for all eternity: "Therefore they are before the throne of God, and serve [worship] him day and night in his temple; and he who sits on the throne will shelter them with his presence." In that place we will never look elsewhere to meet our longing for intimacy and security.

That is God's destination for us. We are still on that journey. So far, we have been focusing on our longings and how they move us now to respond to others in ways that alienate, violate, or truncate relationships. When we treat our need for respect, value, and love as our personal responsibility to acquire, we hinder the flow of the Spirit through us, and we deviate from his path. Pride, idolatry, and unbelief are root sins that thwart our forward progress with God and all our relationships. They can be re-channeled when we live from the resources we received at our new birth. To re-emphasize, Jesus himself lived from the affirmations he received at his baptism. He received the Holy Spirit as the channel of

God's will, character, and power through his life. The Father confirmed his unique identity: "You are my beloved Son," as well as his acceptance and delight in his son: "I am well pleased with you." And because the Spirit of Jesus lives in us, we can live from the same affirmations, no more, no less.

You have been filled with the Holy Spirit.

You are God's child.

Your Father loves you.

Your Father is pleased with you.

He loves you in the same way he loves his Son, because you are part of him. He sees you in the Bride that will wed his Son. You are among those who will fill eternity with your praise and worship of the Living God.

That vision is the unique and sufficient motivation to allow God to be the center of your life, to allow Jesus to be valued and worshiped, to believe that your Father will always take care of you.

3

FROM VALUE TO INSPIRATION

*"When we are securely rooted in personal intimacy with the
source of life, it will be possible to remain flexible without being
relativistic, convinced without being rigid, willing to confront
without being offensive, gentle and forgiving without being soft,
and true witnesses without being manipulative."*
Henri J.M. Nouwen

From the time he was a small boy, Daniel loved attention. The youngest of five siblings, he was inevitably the brunt of rivalries and pranks, but he always found a way to be the center attraction. His older siblings challenged his adolescent need for worship by continually putting him in his place, which only strengthened his resolve to refine his approach, becoming more creative and subtle. Daniel took any opportunity to express himself to a group, act in a play, speak to an audience, get eyes and ears to focus on him. His good looks, Mensa-level intelligence, wit, charm, and emotional awareness gave him the ability to manipulate almost any circumstance to get what felt he needed most: to be idolized and valued. When I met Daniel, he was a sophomore in college, and had already refined his ability to attract personal value to a fine art. At the same time, I saw that he had a sweet, kind heart that instinctively knew the value of other people, and his emotional awareness allowed him to inspire a positive vision of others. Daniel also had a powerful knack for seeing the emotional needs of individuals and groups in conflict and describing those needs in ways that helped each side understand the other and come to a mutually beneficial resolution. This gift of mediation was so effective in Daniel that I suggested he make it the center element of his further education and career planning.

This deep need for value, and the manipulative practice of seeking and siphoning it from others, is the centerpiece of the root sin of idolatry.

This deep need for value, and the manipulative practice of seeking and siphoning it from others, is the centerpiece of the root sin of idolatry. Just as a pride-based person viscerally hates failure, being wrong, being incompetent, not having clarity, and not being respected, an idolater is deeply incensed when they feel devalued: insignificant, not listened to or heard, misunderstood, or second-guessed. Whether they are aware of it or not, they enter almost every conversation or situation seeking a way to vacuum value from it, often with deception or manipulation. All of us are inclined to speak and act in ways that show others what we want them to see or what we believe they want to see about us. We do this in order to appear competent, receive approval, get something we want, or to avoid a conflict. Idolaters are more masterful at creating these façades, so much so that without their willingness to be transparent, almost no one will become aware of their deceit nor ever know their true identity. They will feel the most frustrated and painful emotions when they are thwarted in their attempts to gain value, or when someone with a different root sin is unaware or unwilling to meet their need.

I have seen the root sin of idolatry play out vividly in several fields, among politicians, actors, musicians, church leaders, business owners, and athletes. My young friend, Kyle, is very intelligent, deeply empathetic, and acutely aware of the emotional situation of everyone around him. He is also talented musician and thoughtful communicator, all of which make him, among other things, a skillful worship leader. One morning I was watching him lead his worship band in a final rehearsal before the morning services, and I was grateful and proud of how well he could use his skills to bring the best musicianship out of each instrument and singer, all the while making sure each person felt valued. This inspired the value of the entire band. As the service began, the lights went down in the room, and Kyle stepped up to lead us in worship. At that moment, something shifted in him. Maybe it was the reality of having several hundred of his peers focused on him at once or the sense of control he felt as the director of the moment. He moved into the spotlight, he became the center of attention, he began to draw value from the room. Of course, he skillfully led us in singing worship songs that he and the band supported musically from a place of humility. My guess is that few, if any, saw what was happening in Kyle, the incongruence that he veiled, the unnoticed satisfaction he was gaining. Only because I knew him and his struggle so well could I see what was happening in his heart. His need for value was so powerful, and that situation was so ripe for his picking, that even with the intentions of leading a worship service, Kyle could not step out of the spotlight. He and I talked about how the root sin of idolatry had painted a patina over his heart so that he presented what would attract his friends' desire for him. Kyle realized that he would need to stop leading worship for a season. This gave him space to see the strength of his entitlement for value and how much energy he put into crafting his image. After moving into another area, and becoming a member of a loving community where he could be authentic, Kyle began releasing his need to draw value from others. At work, in church, and with his family, he consistently sees and inspires the value of the people around him.

Jesus saw the God-created value of everyone he encountered, whether or not they were willing to acknowledge it in themselves or others.

This is the journey toward the character of Jesus. He saw the God-created value of everyone he encountered, whether or not they were willing to acknowledge it in themselves or others. We see Jesus expressing his deepest compassion or passionate disapproval in the face of unrecognized value. He was known for enjoying a meal with those his culture rejected and for calling out the religious leaders who encouraged their rejection. Although he knew everyone's heart most clearly, he refused to judge them and instead encouraged them to see themselves and God from the right lens. He knew they were unguided sheep, but he loved them because his Father loved them and was calling them back to him. As C. S. Lewis reminds us, the most holy thing you will see this side of heaven is the person sitting next to you. Jesus knew at whom he looked, and he inspired God's children to display what he had created in them.

This is the redeemed side of idolatry. We drop our entitlement to being heard, understood, and significant, which vacuums value from every conversation, social event, and meeting we attend. We refuse to feed our addiction to personal significance, to manufacture and preen our façade, to manipulate opinions and impressions. When the Spirit turns our hearts away from our own pursuit of value and shows us what our Father really thinks of us, we can flow in his power with his vision for the people around us. He shows us how to be intentional in each conversation, how to listen for him to tell us what he sees, why he delights in others, and what he wants to highlight in their hearts. We shift from being a spokesperson for our own merits and accomplishments, and we become advocates of another's passions.

Think about how this shift in perspective and purpose would affect your relationships. If you often find yourself in conflict because you believe you are unheard, unappreciated, or devalued, pause and examine how that perception is making you feel and how you are reflecting that to the other person. Do you feel inadequate, insecure, insignificant, or something else? Is that emotion causing a desire to turn the conversation toward you, to demand overtly or covertly to be seen and heard? Are you tempted to hijack the conversation in some way to highlight the significance of your experience or achievement? Ultimately, are you tempted to see another person, as they express their views and knowledge as a threat to your value or as a gift to be valued? Now ask the Spirit how he sees the situation. Why do you so desperately need to be heard right now? Are you willing to drop that entitlement and listen with the intent to know what others need? If you do that with increasing regularity, you will begin to see your conversations become more fruitful, and your relationships will start to thrive rather than wither. You will also see how your personal gifts enhance your groups and communities, because you now contribute what the Spirit has for them. You also become an inspiration for others to drop their own entitlements, see each other as gifts rather than threats, and focus on what God is doing among you.

IDOLATRY

I feel like I'm worthless, unheard, and misunderstood

I want to be significant

I need to be valued

I use manipulation to get worship

I am deceptive

But...

I am not entitled to value

I am filled with the Spirit

He brings me to submission

He shows me his heart

So...

I inspire people to authentic worship

INSPIRATION

INTERLUDE
PHILIPPIANS 2 – ENTITLEMENTS AND THE CROSS

That's not fair! Hey, that's mine! What's in this for me? I deserve it! Get your own! It's not your turn! Why should I? She has to apologize first! You never listen to me... You don't care...

Words from a playground? A high school cafeteria? A dinner table? A divorce lawyer's office? Possibly. More likely, they occurred in the heart, unspoken before ever being expressed. These, and many others, are the phrases of entitlement. Our unredeemed humanity lives from a place of self-preservation, self-aggrandizement, and self-focus, which rip apart the trust and intimacy that our relationships and communities need to thrive. Paul's exhortation rings into the very center of our self-orientation: "Do nothing from selfish ambition or conceit, but in humility count others more significant than yourselves." More significant than me? I'm addicted to my own significance. I've spent most of my life one way or the other trying to get everyone to recognize how significant I am. So have you. Why would we want to change that now?

If I am reading Paul correctly here, his contention is that there is something more satisfying, more meaningful, a unity of being part of Christ together that requires us to reset our minds and hearts toward each other: "having the same mind, having the same love, being in full accord and of one mind." He provides us with two motivations for choosing to refocus: what Christ has provided us and what Christ has done for us. We have "encouragement in Christ," "comfort from love," "participation in the Spirit," namely, Christ fully satisfies us spiritually and emotionally in our relationship with him. We no longer need to secretly turn the attentions and affections of others toward filling our need for significance.

Then we have, in its mystery and generosity, the most stunning example of self-sacrifice known to history. You can feel the awe and gratitude in Paul's voice as he speaks of the heart attitude of Christ Jesus, refusing to cling to his equality with God, completely releasing himself into the human body of a servant, lowering himself to the ultimate humility of death on a cross. Jesus accepted multiple acts of torture, all the while knowing he was entitled to the exaltation of the highest name, the universal veneration of every bowing knee, the confession of his Lordship by every tongue. God's son chose to receive these from his Father, rather than sweep them up alone. Our own attempts at self-protection and self-promotion suddenly seem ridiculous, almost blasphemous.

God breaks the power of my entitlement to respect, and with it my drive to being right, to clarity, to success, by bringing me to the scene of Jesus' cross. In the vision of Jesus' battered body hanging on spikes nailed through him into a rough tree, the Father asks me some simple questions.

Who is the one human in all the universe who unquestionably deserves to be respected? Who is always right, always crystal clear, never a failure? He gave up his right to respect to hang up there.

Who is the one being who has the character, power, glory, righteousness to be justly worshipped by all of creation? He gave up his glory and worship to hang up there.

Who is the one person in the world who is defined as love and who rightfully draws all people to love him first? He is abandoned and unloved hanging up there.

God's son, Jesus, was entitled to all respect, value, and love, from all and everything in his creation. In order to receive something better, in order to be able to give something better, for the joy set before him, for the redemption of all creation, for the shame-free and sin-free relationship with his children, for the glory, righteousness, and justice of the Father, for the filling and flowing of the Spirit into our hearts, Jesus laid down his entitlements. He even gave up his entitlement to life itself.

Jesus laid down his entitlements. He even gave up his entitlement to life itself.

When you experience sudden loss or threat of loss to your respect, your value, or your love, immediately hold them out to Jesus. Only when you drop your entitlements can you receive and give what the Spirit has for you and others that will sustain the flourishing relationship your Father wants.

4

From Love to Peacemaking

"I am sorry I ran from you. I am still running, running from that knowledge, that eye, that love from which there is no refuge. For you meant only love, and love, and I felt only fear, and pain. So once in Israel love came to us incarnate, stood in the doorway between two worlds, and we were all afraid."
Annie Dillard

I first met Bryan along with a group of his friends. He didn't say much that night, nor during the next couple of times I spent with that group. I noticed he was well liked by his peers, very engaged, and polite to a fault. His intelligent demeanor and likeable personality sparked my curiosity, and I invited him to get coffee with me. Over our first conversation, I learned that Bryan grew up in a small town, that he was adept at sports, and that his achievements were high enough to land a full scholarship to a major university. As a freshman, he started off in the fraternity party scene, but a couple years in he realized that was helping neither his heart nor his grades, so he connected with a healthier friend group. He worked hard and achieved well in a challenging college major. Over our subsequent conversations, I noticed that Bryan would often express his progress in school, relationships, or decision making in terms of fear or anxiety. He needed to behave in a way that would avoid disapproval or rejection from his friends and instructors. I could see that Bryan was intelligent, capable, and teachable. He had significant personal influence among his peers and enormous leadership potential. At the same time, he demonstrated a paralyzing lack of confidence in himself. During much of his college career, rather that reach out and engage others with his gifts, he would often choose to isolate himself. Decisions about relationships or career opportunities came only after a long period of self-doubt and swirling uncertainty.

As I watched this dichotomy unfold in Bryan's heart and life, I realized that he was living out of some powerful entitlements. Fundamentally, he believed that he would lose relationships and be unloved and alone if he did not please others and avoid causing conflict. He needed to protect himself and everyone around him from pain and discomfort. This made it frightening to reach out to someone without knowing what they might approve or disapprove of about him. This made any major decision process excruciating because of unknown factors he might not be able to control. As real as these motivations were, Bryan was only implicitly aware of them. He knew he often felt anxious or dissatisfied, but he wasn't clear about how to become more free.

We realized there was also a spiritual component constraining him. Bryan needed to know that his identity is rooted, just like for Jesus, in what his Father God says: you are my beloved son. His heart longed to be secure in the truth that his Father is ultimately pleased with him; he created Bryan as a son, and he gave his own Son for his life. Bryan did not need to strive for the approval of everyone around him but could reach out to them knowing that whatever they thought of him, he was secure in his Father's love. Another reality for Bryan was what he believed about the Father's commitment to taking care of him in every relationship and endeavor. He lived from a fear that if he did not control his circumstances himself and ensure he pleased people, he would be abandoned. In a deep place, Jesus was not good enough for Bryan; Bryan had to make up the difference himself. Shame was lying to Bryan and telling him that he wasn't worth that kind of commitment from God. The Father's heart is just the opposite. I asked Bryan to begin walking into every conversation and decision with these words: "My Father is pleased with me, and I am pleased with my Father." These two truths are the antidote to fear and anxiety in the face of unbelief. When we drop our entitlement to creating love and relationship ourselves, we can receive the love and relationship of our Father and allow the Spirit to flow those into the ones he loves around us.

The tempter caused Eve to entertain the possibility that God had a hidden agenda, that he wasn't to be trusted.

The root sin of unbelief revolves around this fundamental need to be loved and not abandoned. Often without really being aware of it, there is doubt: God's love and his commitment to care for us are uncertain. This started in the Garden of Eden. The tempter caused Eve to entertain the possibility that God had a hidden agenda, that he wasn't to be trusted, that she and Adam needed to take things into their own hands. Doubt flowed throughout the history of Israel, into the story of Jesus, and it challenged the formation and development of the Church. At the personal level, people driven by unbelief demonstrate doubt in all their relationships: they will often feel disliked, uncared for, or afraid, even with little outside evidence. So, they instinctively avoid pain, discomfort, and conflict, for themselves and for everyone around them. They can also take up a personal responsibility to protect other people from pain and find those deeply offensive who cause pain and discomfort. In the world of unbelief, conflict is nearly always bad and should be avoided if at all possible. There is a visceral need to be liked, which results in people pleasing, either actively or passively. All this from a root of doubt about God's character and motives.

When the Spirit makes us aware of our unbelief, he takes us on a path to drop our entitlements to being pain-free, comfortable, liked, and in safe relationships. These are all gifts that our loving Father may grant us, but when we demand them and manipulate our world to secure them, we create chaos in ourselves and others. The Spirit transforms our awareness of discomfort and pain, our need for love and safe relationships, our sensitivity to conflict. He does this with his desire to bring peace between us, God, and one another. Jesus promises us his peace, and he flows his peace through those who have discovered how to meet their need for comfort, security, and safety in their relationship with him. When we learn to listen to the Spirit in the midst of our discomfort or insecurity, he can turn that sensitivity toward others, allowing us to know that for which their hearts long and how to become a peacemaker who brings them together and to Christ. Just as the Spirit transforms pride into wisdom and idolatry into inspiration, he moves us from unbelief to peace, to becoming ones who bring the peace of Jesus to hurting, doubting hearts.

The Spirit moves us from unbelief to peace, to becoming ones who bring the peace of Jesus.

I've watched this happen in the life of my friend and ministry partner, Dennis. When I met Dennis in 1991, he was the poster child for the root sin of unbelief (as I was for pride), although we had not yet developed those categories for explaining our relationships. As we took different directions with our training and career paths, we have maintained a close relationship. Over more than two decades, we have mutually developed our skills and passion in managing conflict and mediation, in both personal and organizational situations. Our styles are very different, but they mesh effectively. Dennis likes to describe my approach to conflict as "blunt force trauma" and his as "the stiletto." If the conflict is noisy or violent, my pride-based perspective moves quickly to clarity and to working out an effective strategy for immediate change. When the conflict is more measured or deeply hurtful, the need Dennis has for comfort moves furtively toward felt needs and heart awareness. Early in the process of working together in mediation, our root sins clashed, and we often felt undercut by each other. I would see emotionally abusive or violent communication, and I would suggest an immediate, direct approach. Dennis would counter with his desire to move more carefully, understanding the underlying needs without causing too much pain. Our relationship is important to us, so we worked on seeing the situation from the other's perspective. I learned how important Dennis's sensitivity to pain is in helping a hurting heart trust an approaching healer. Dennis has seen my ability to bring clarity and wisdom into a confusing mix of emotional noise. We have come to trust our gifts and insight, and we don't need to compete with each other. We can use our different abilities to support and contribute to the overall movement of a conflict to healing and intimacy. By allowing the Spirit to transform our pride and unbelief, Dennis brings peace and wisdom into places of confusion and pain, and he leads others to Jesus as the ultimate source for their needs.

UNBELIEF

I feel unliked, uncared for, and afraid

I want to be pain free

I need to be comfortable

I try to please people

I am paralyzed

But...

I am not entitled to comfort nor to being pain-free

I am filled with the Spirit

He brings me to faith

He leads me to his peace

So...

I bring the presence of Christ

PEACE

INTERLUDE
MATTHEW 4 – THE TEMPTER

"I've got to get rid of this smart phone. I swear I'm trading it in for a flip phone. Social media is just too tempting. It's too easy for me to go online and find another woman to hook up with." It was a statement of resolve that reflected ongoing recovery, counting the cost of consequences previously ignored. My friend is about two years into the new lifestyle he adopted when he left behind a decade of parties, drugs, alcohol, and uncountable sexual connections, from one-time acts with strangers and casual liaisons to more serious relationships. He is valiantly pursuing a path toward health and freedom, which is why we were talking. He no longer depends on substances and physical pleasure to fulfill his needs for connection and intimacy, yet, I was aware that his heart was not free and that he was emotionally walled off. With further conversation, I realized that he had dozens of unreleased spiritual and emotional connections in his heart to his past, from those he harmed and those who had harmed him. These relational hooks in his heart pulled him away from intimacy with God and his community, and they pulled him back into shame and temptation. We both knew that this is not where Jesus wanted him to remain, so we asked Jesus to walk up to each hook and remove it. Through honest interaction with Jesus over these individuals, groups, and painful events, my friend's heart found release, reconciliation, and freedom. In the midst of a desire for holiness and submission, Jesus' compassion, mercy, forgiveness, and grace restored what the enemy had stolen.

As we approach the possibility of an encounter between Jesus and our brokenness, we often have to make a painful and scary choice. Will we allow Jesus to come into a place that we have kept closed off, maybe from very early in our lives? What would motivate us to risk that kind of exposure? If only we knew that he understood us and how we have succumbed to our weaknesses. If only we knew his way with us would be merciful. From the stories of Jesus' life, we have these very assurances.

The voice of Jesus' Father was still echoing around him, "You are my son. I love you. I am very pleased with you." After three decades of learning Scripture and the voice of God, now baptized and filled with the Spirit, absolutely clear about his identity as God's son, Jesus was prepared for his ministry to begin. Save one more test, maybe not for him alone, but for his tempter as well. Under the Spirit's leading, he walked from the Jordan riverbank into the arid, rock-strewn hills beyond the borders of Palestinian civilization and the presence of anyone except the devil. For forty days and nights, he took in no food to sustain his body. While he does not share with us any of the encounters he had with his Father or the tempter, it does seem that Jesus' time in the wilderness strengthened his resolve to fulfill God's purpose. After six weeks of fasting, the tempter sought to take advantage of his physical weakness. By coming into the created order as a man, Jesus marked an end to Satan's long reign of death and destruction. Knowing this well, Satan made one last ditch effort to lure God's son away from his father and his purpose, just as he had successfully done to Adam and Eve in the Garden of Eden. He even addresses the very same root sins.

After forty days without food, Jesus is hungry. Satan knows who he is, of what he is capable, and from where his power comes. "You and I both know that you are the Son of God, and that you can do basically anything you want to do. You would really like to eat, so make yourself some bread out of these stones here." It seems like a simple thing. And Jesus knows how to do it; he would later feed several thousand people from a few pieces of fish and bread. He also knows there is far more at stake here than sating his personal hunger. His basic task is to reverse the consequences the first couple caused by acting out of their independence from God. The serpent had told Adam and Eve that by eating of the forbidden tree they would become like God, knowing good and evil. Satan was making a play at Jesus for the same hubris: act outside of your relationship with God, and prove you know what you're doing. Unlike Eve, however, Jesus isn't taken in by this temptation. He knows what God said about the manna he provided to an earlier generation of his people in the wilderness: "when you were hungry, I gave you this strange food to eat with specific instructions on how to receive it so that you would know that I am committed to taking care of you when you choose to heed what I tell you." Jesus refused to act from pride: he did not need to prove his competence or demand respect for his miraculous powers. He submitted himself to his Father's calling and purpose.

When Satan saw that Jesus would not succumb to pride, he moved on to unbelief: "We both know that God is committed to protecting his children. In fact, in one of your own precious

Psalms, God says that his angels will guard you and carry you away from harm. So, let's give it a try. It's a pretty long drop from the top of the temple up here, so jump into those angel arms and let them fly you down. That will definitely prove to everyone that you are the Messiah." Jesus, however, knew that God's faithfulness did not need this kind of a test, and so he tells the tempter. Jesus had no doubt in his Father's ability or desire to protect his son. Unlike Adam and Eve, Jesus knew that the liar in this situation was Satan, not God. There is also no evidence that Jesus lived from an entitlement to comfort or safety, nor sought to please anyone but his Father. Anxiety and fear had no place in him. He knew his Father's heart for him. Nothing would happen to Jesus outside of the Father's control. He knew the faith that keeps us in an eternal relationship with God believes in both God's character and his sovereignty.

In one last effort, the devil pushed on the third root sin: idolatry. "Ok, Son of God, come with me, let me show you what I have for you. Look at all those glorious kingdoms in the world over which I have authority. I will gladly cede my control and ownership to you. Only one thing is necessary: bow before me in worship, and it's all yours." It's hard to believe that Satan did not know what a ridiculous prospect that was. Both he and Jesus had been in the presence of the God of the Universe in all his glorious majesty and splendor, unapproachable light, pure holiness, unrivaled power and authority. Both of them had experienced the deafening euphony of worship from heavenly beings created expressly to praise their King. Jesus' response in the face of such indignity was rapid and fierce: "Get out of my sight this instant, Deceiver! I will worship only my God and Father!" Satan obeyed, for the time being; three years hence Jesus would crush the head of that serpent.

Jesus knew that he was God; he could have demanded value and worship, even forced people to bow in his presence. He instead submitted to his Father's word and will; he did and said only what the Father showed him. He glorified God, and he lifted up those who had lost their dignity. Seeing him inspire hope and value in tax collectors, prostitutes, lepers, demoniacs, widows, grieving parents and friends, even dead people, are among the poignant scenes in Jesus' life.

The author of Hebrews spotlights our benefit from Jesus' resistance in the face of pride, idolatry, and unbelief: "For we do not have a high priest who is unable to sympathize with our weaknesses, but one who in every respect has been tempted as we are, yet without sin. Let us then with confidence draw near to the throne of grace, that we may receive mercy and find grace to help in time of need."

5

INTERACTING LONGINGS
THE INTERPLAY OF FULFILLMENT

"God did not make this person as I would have made him. He did not give him to me as a brother for me to dominate and control, but in order that I might find above him the Creator. Now the other person, in the freedom with which he was created, becomes the occasion of joy, whereas before he was only a nuisance and an affliction. God does not will that I should fashion the other person according to the image that seems good to me, that is, in my own image; rather in his very freedom from me God made this person in His image. I can never know beforehand how God's image should appear in others. That image always manifests a completely new and unique form that comes solely from God's free and sovereign creation. To me the sight may seem strange, even ungodly. But God creates every man in the likeness of His Son, the Crucified. After all, even that image certainly looked strange and ungodly to me before I grasped it."
Dietrich Bonhoeffer

One of the more valuable aspects of becoming aware of root sins is seeing the way they affect all of your relationships. How you engage with everyone in your life is a product of your own needs and entitlements and how you submit those to the Spirit. Begin noticing how your parents, your siblings, your friends, your partners, your workmates respond to each other and to you. When you are confronted, what is triggered in you? Why do you think another person responds the way he or she does? What seems to be the underlying need in a passionate emotional scene? Why does someone suddenly go quiet and withdraw from a conversation? Does it seem that one of your friends needs to be right all the time? Does your boss look dissatisfied when one his ideas is unappreciated? Why does your mother seem to take her role a bit too seriously? These kinds of observations are not meant to foster judgment. They are a necessary to love the way Jesus does. He understands the deep-seated needs of every heart, and he draws them under his care and power. He desires to move his children together and to mesh their gifts into unity. Each of the root sins I have described consistently responds to stress, pain, confrontation, and loss in its unique manner. A pride-based person will have a different effect on another pride-based person than she will on an idolatry-based or un-belief-based person. Some examples will illustrate.

Let's say you are a pride-based person, and your wife is unbelief based (the situation for me and Debbie). If you have not been introduced to those ideas, you manage your relationship mostly from a place of vague confusion, as we did for the better part of our marriage. You know that you love each other, and you want your relationship to flourish. At the same time, whenever you engage in the smaller details of life, or the decisions that affect the future of your family, you spend a lot of emotional energy trying to understand why your partner does not think the way you do. Are your values really that different? Did you somehow start speaking a different language after your honeymoon? Did one of you finally reveal that you are really from another planet? (I seem to recall something about Mars and Venus.) No, what actually is happening is you are both responding to each other from your yet-to-be-identified entitlements.

**God desires to move his children together
and to mesh their gifts into unity.**

When Johnny brings home a note from his teacher telling you that he is isolated and seems to be having trouble making friends, both of you react in different ways. You, the pride-based person, immediately want to confront Johnny and find out why he is refusing to make friends. His failure taps your failure. You can sense the teacher's implicit disrespect for your parenting skills, and you demand immediate clarity to fix the problem. Your wife, the unbelief-based person, senses the powerful discomfort of conflict, and is horrified by the idea of you confronting your son in that way. She wants to protect Johnny from both his peers and his father. Johnny is already feeling uncomfortable with his other relationships; it is paramount that he feels safe in his relationship with his mother, and you get thrown under the bus. In this scenario, your conflict management styles take over. Even though you may not understand or value the other person's approach to the problem, you will resort to the way you have reacted in the past: win, lose, or compromise. An understanding of your needs and entitlements is necessary for breakthrough. If you drop your entitlement to clarity and respect, if your wife drops her entitlement to comfort and relationship, and if you both listen to each other and the Spirit for what you and Johnny need, there is an opportunity to bring God's wisdom and peace into the situation. In the noise of the conflict, that kind of listening will seem difficult, so start with quieting your emotions and releasing your need to control the discussion. There is a way to hear each other and Johnny and to allow the Spirit to bring compassion and grace over each of you.

Lisa is in her mid-twenties, in her first job out of college, living in a city several hours away from her hometown. She came seeking help for her recurring depression. From the outset, it was evident that Lisa thought of herself and her ideas as superior. In fact, she already thought she knew what she needed to treat her depression. She described her family's opinion of their own excellence, mostly revealed through inference and critique of others. Their message was, "Respectable people work hard, don't brag, and, above all, are not fat and out of shape." Her family made sport of criticizing others in support of their own superiority. Roots of pride and idolatry spread throughout their interactions. Depression, therefore, was a sign of weakness and failure. Lisa's mother, a well-known and respected physician, took it upon herself to the shape her daughter into a competent, self-reliant young woman, while communicating in manipulative and harmful ways. Lisa described conversations with her mother as defeating and demoralizing; her mother devalued her ideas and rarely conceded to her point of view, even when it was about her work. Lisa felt confused and lost. Her mother's passive manner of downplaying Lisa's challenges and critiquing her thoughts evoked pain and failure in Lisa's heart. In all of this, Lisa did not blame or accuse her mother, but assumed her mother's lack of affirmation as evidence of Lisa's inadequacy. Lisa thought that determined hard work would solve her problem. She needed to prove to her family that she was respectable and worthy of their pride in her. At work, Lisa rebuffed criticism, blaming incompetent co-workers who refused to accept her ideas. She hid any ignorance and avoided asking for help. Viciously self-critical, Lisa felt only the deep disrespect of failure. This permeated all her relationships, and convinced her that she could only be tolerated. It took empathy and persistent truth for Lisa to realize the strength of her entitlements to success and respect, and how much her fear of failure drove her interactions. Distance from her family dynamics helped her see other opinions and ideas were not threats to her competence. Her need to be right softened into compassion that helped people from her abilities. She learned to accept her identity and gifts, without needing to prove herself to her family, and she went on to explore a vocation that meshed with her real interests. Eventually she was able to overcome the shame her family communicated, accept the reality of her depression, and receive the care she needed to recover.

Steve and Molly are both young physicians, competent, respected, and successful in their disciplines, employed at a prestigious university medical center. They are both competitive high achievers; results at the highest level have always been expected without question. They were referred to me, because, in spite of their professional success, they were failing in their relationship with each other, and for any number of reasons, this was deemed unacceptable. They had both come from families where exceptional achievement was encouraged and expected. They had been married for several years, and they clearly loved each other. They were also committed to learning how to relate and to communicate more effectively so their relationship could thrive. At the same time, their pride-based approach to life and relationships was thwarting the intimacy and security they desired. They both demanded clarity, but in different ways and for different reasons. As normal life stress and challenges devolved into conflict, each of them reacted from skewed perceptions of the other. As I listened to them describe their interactions, although Steve was more aggressive, and Molly was more anxious, I realized they both lived from an entitlement to avoid failure at any cost. At the same time, Steve had a deep need for relational intimacy, and Molly could become nearly hysterical when she did not feel secure, so they both spent a lot of emotional energy on manipulating their worlds to gain control. Over several conversations, we were able to identify these entitlements and recognize the power they had over their relationship. Of course we first had to lower the emotional noise, remove violent language, and silence the lies shame was telling them so they each could see their hearts. Eventually, Steve learned that Molly's emotions were not a threat to his competence or respect, and to focus on the needs and expectations that were driving them. Molly learned that Steve's desire for intimacy was not a threat to her success, and her family was not a source of competition for her career. The challenge they continue to face is how their individual entitlements filter through their upbringing and personality types.

I met Ryan and Ashley on a Sunday morning at the church where they led worship. Ryan was part of a community of other young men that I mentored, but I had yet to meet him. I was the guest speaker that morning, and after the service we got acquainted. Eventually, I began meeting with Ryan, and when he and Ashley were engaged, Debbie and I performed their pre-marital counseling. Both of them are intelligent, wise, caring people with multiple life experiences and accomplishments. They are beloved by their family and friends, and they have a seriously positive impact on their world. In our conversations, it did not take long to notice that both Ryan and Ashley operated from the place of unbelief. They struggled individually to make life decisions, they were less than fully confident in their identity, they backed away from conflict. Although they had been dating for more than two years, it took Ashley many months to overcome her fear that she would not be good at being Ryan's wife and that she would not like being married. Ryan was the new owner of a small business, and while he was successful at building community among his clients, he struggled to keep up with the ongoing decision making each day required, especially in email correspondence. Clearing his inbox was a monumental task as he agonized over every response to make sure he did not displease someone. They had a mature, loving relationship and a strong desire to grow more intimate. Because of their mutual emotional sensitivity, they tended to transfer their anxiety to each other, and then be disappointed that they were hurting the other person. Their strong need to not lose relationships, to be loved and safe, kept them from hearing the truth about their identity, and living from a place of confidence. In ongoing conversations with them, we talked about believing God's voice rather than the voice of shame. They learned to hear of his acceptance and confidence in them, their adequacy for each other, and the gifts he wanted to channel through them. The temptation to doubt God and themselves and to fear losing a relationship is still real, but they know how to walk through pain and discomfort toward peace.

The advantage of understanding the root sins paradigm is how effectively it can cut through the emotional noise and shame to see the most powerful motivators.

These types of emotional and spiritual issues are common in relationships, marriages, and organizations. Counselors of all types walk people through these challenges regularly. The advantage of understanding the root sins paradigm is how effectively it can cut through the emotional noise and shame to see the most powerful motivators underneath that smoke-screen. Of course emotions are real and powerful, of course shame whispers and shouts its half-truths, of course we have learned to speak violently without compassion and empathy toward each other. The critical question is why? Why do we have such powerful emotional responses? Why do we believe what shame tells us about ourselves and others? Why do we push and shove our way around in conversations? While the answer involves a complexity of factors, fundamentally it begins at the core of our heart, where our deepest needs go disregarded, disapproved, and unmet. Then the sin of pride, idolatry, or unbelief starts demanding and turns the needs into entitlements. We know that the biblical antidote to sin is blood-bought grace, accessed through confession, forgiveness, and repentance and lived out in submission to the Spirit. These are all part of the action we take when we drop our entitlements and allow ourselves to become channels of the Spirit. This process is not meant to truncate the empathy and compassion we need to lower the emotional noise and silence shame. Nor is it meant to diminish the courage necessary to challenge violence head-on. Understanding and addressing the fundamental reality of root sins actually empowers grace and freedom to make higher-level healing effective and permanent.

INTERLUDE
GENESIS 3 – THE TREE

A lush garden. A forbidden tree. A naked woman. A talking serpent. A fateful decision.

Questions abound. Is this the plotline of some ancient myth? Why did there need to be a tree of the knowledge of good and evil in such a nice garden, especially given its deadly fruit? Why was a contrary serpent allowed there? Where was Adam? Where was God? From what we can tell, they were both aware of this conversation. Why did they not intervene? It almost sounds like a setup.

In some ways, it was. God's desire is a relationship with his children built on their mutual, uncoerced loyalty; true intimacy requires trust that goes both ways. He put a tree of life and a tree of death in the garden, and he allowed his children to choose. He wanted to demonstrate his character and love in his own actions and see it in the ones he created in his image. An infinitely glorious God glorifies what he makes so he can be glorified by it. As the storyline continues, we see that God made provision even for this failure; we are on a journey back to glory, his and ours.

True intimacy requires trust that goes both ways.

So, from the perspective of Scripture, everything happening in the world around us can be explained from one conversation between a woman and a serpent. As mythical, even fantastic, as that sounds, even Jesus himself affirms it. Had that interaction in the Garden of Eden gone differently, we would not be having this discussion. Everything we know about human pain and misery, war, death, injustice, bigotry, abuse, hatred, destruction, and depravation would not exist. There is no reliable explanation from biology, quantum physics, evolution, sociology, or psychology that can address our instinctual refusal to respect, value, and love each other and the world around us. Every parent can attest to the self-oriented, independent bent of their children almost from birth; the rebellion of Eden is evidently built into us.

The description of how Eve (and Adam) made her decision to disobey God highlights our three fundamental entitlements. When the tempter raised the possibility of God's duplicity—"Did God actually say...?"—Eve initially responded (somehow not batting an eye at the prospect of a talking serpent) with her understanding of the consequences God had warned. Why she was taken in by the liar's subsequent reinterpretation of God's words is an eternal mystery. Why was she willing to question God's intentions? It seems almost sudden, almost like she was waiting for an excuse to have what was forbidden to her. With Adam looking over her shoulder, doubt turned to unbelief, the beauty and sustenance of the tree became idolatry, a desire for God-like wisdom birthed pride. Even as Adam and Eve chewed their first bite of the poisonous fruit, the curtain of guilt and shame fell over them. What was freedom, pleasure, and joy at once felt embarrassing, frightening, wrong. So the hiding began, from each other and from God.

These three root sins, pride, idolatry, and unbelief, permeate the Bible's storyline. God's relationship with his people and his persistence in their redemption are framed by these fundamental forces. Every relationship, every action in the story is marked by the interplay or the overcoming of this brokenness in the human heart. When our felt needs for respect, value, and love move from gifts we receive to demands we grab, our entitlements clash with each other, conflict erupts, and relationships splinter. When we become aware of our unredeemed motivations and submit them to the Spirit, we can drop our entitlements and allow our gifts to flow toward the other person. I recognize this is difficult to do in the face to noisy emotions, abusive or violent communication, and identity-crushing shame. Difficult, but not impossible. There are tools to overcome those challenges: to quiet the noise, remove the violence, silence the shame, and channel the Spirit, which we will discuss as this series progresses. In the meantime, notice how much closer you can move toward someone when you focus on their need first.

One of the most encouraging aspects of the biblical storyline is the constant movement toward God's redemption. There are many twists and turns, but there is a single focus on one person and the actions he would perform to make it happen. From the moment Adam and Eve were thrust out of the Garden of Eden, history flowed toward the Redeemer, Jesus Christ. In his first coming to earth, he lived perfectly, died sacrificially, and rose up victoriously over the great deceiver. Now as he refines his people, and calls the rest of his children home, we wait for Jesus to return a final time to complete the recovery effort. The story culminates with the rebuilding of the dwelling place of God with his people, a new heaven and earth, with a new city to fulfill all that Eden was meant to provide. And there is a tree in the middle of it again—only one this time: a tree of life:

"Then the angel showed me the river of the water of life, bright as crystal, flowing from the throne of God and of the Lamb through the middle of the street of the city; also, on either side of the river, the tree of life with its twelve kinds of fruit, yielding its fruit each month. The leaves of the tree were for the healing of the nations. No longer will here be anything accursed, but the throne of God and of the Lamb will be in it, and his servants will worship him. They will see his face, and his name will be on their foreheads. And night will be no more. They will need no light of lamp or sun, for the Lord God will be their light, and they will reign forever and ever." – Revelation 22:1-5

CONCLUSION
A LIFE OF REDEEMED LONGINGS

Your relationships, with God and with others, will either flourish or flounder based on how well you know your own heart. There is a lot to discover there: spiritual awareness, emotional intelligence, neurobiology, relational skills, conflict style, personality traits, and the effects of trauma, abuse, and shame. Dennis and I will address ways to navigate some of those areas in the next books. As we created the tools we have used foster healthy relationships and build leaders over the course of two decades, we realized that this one idea needed to be unpacked first.

Root sins are fundamental to our unredeemed beings, and exist throughout our development until they are transformed by the Spirit. They will show up differently in our various relationships, based on how we are raised and taught. They are different from our personality types, although they will be filtered through our individual personalities and appear in various ways. For example, in their wonderful children's story, *The Treasure Tree*, John Trent and Gary Smalley use four animals to categorize our relational styles: Lion, Beaver, Golden Retriever, and Otter. The Lion insists he knows where he's going and wants to lead, the Beaver needs to keep everything organized, the Golden Retriever wants to make sure everyone is feeling good, and the Otter just wants to have a great time. A pride-based Lion is fully understandable, but are there unbelief-based Lions? (Are you thinking *The Wizard of Oz*?) An idolatry-based Otter seems plausible, but what of a Golden Retriever who siphons value out of helping people? Our entitlements will filter through our personality and manifest in some unique ways. Those who have experienced abuse, trauma, or mental illness will sometimes demonstrate unusual or hyperbolic responses to pain that require specialized care. Again, our role is not to label and judge but to recognize and empathize and to reach out for any help we need.

The crucible for working out our understanding of root sins and their implications is, of course, our closest relationships. To reinforce the idea from Chapter Five, think through your childhood and recognize why some of you always had to be right, why others always championed their significance, why some avoided confrontations and tried to referee when they happened. Did your father push you toward success at sports or in school? Was your mother really good at mothering? Look at your work situation and notice who always needs more clarity, who hates to be second guessed, how long it takes another group to make a decision. In the history of your romantic relationships, the ones that lasted and the ones that moved apart, when did you feel the most loved and cared for? What made your conversations productive, and how did they turn into conflicts? Over time you will learn how to recognize why you are encouraged or hurt in a conversation why you receive gratitude or grief when you engage someone. From that point you can listen to the Spirit, as he speaks from his word, and from his presence in you, you may discover what the other person needs and what part you have in meeting that need.

Debbie, my unbelief-based wife, has learned to slow down my pride-based freight train to comprehension and competence with a simple reminder that I just might not get clarity on this one. She also remembers to ask someone a few more questions than she needs the answers to, because she knows I will want the information. She has come to respond less out of fear, and she often takes on some prophetic courage to move an uncomfortable conflict toward peace.

On my side, I have learned that being right is different from making sure everyone else knows I'm right. I still hate to be lost when I'm travelling, but I have submitted to GPS technology rather than demand clarity from my (to remain unnamed) human navigator who struggles with map reading. If I choose to listen to the Spirit in a conversation or a meeting, even when my pride button is being pushed, he consistently shows me how he wants understanding and wisdom to play out. He channels our gifts and abilities to bring people together and bring them to Jesus.

Both Dennis and I have seen the benefit of the root sin paradigm in multiple situations: personal and group counseling, marriage and family dynamics, classroom management, organizational conflicts, leadership development, board rooms, cross-cultural ministry, and more. It is universally helpful because it recognizes how to move us from living merely as children of Adam to flourishing as children of God. Our three paths out of Paradise transform into the way to return.

Discussion Questions

From Tolerated to Treasured

- By whom in life do you feel treasured?

- Are there relationships in which you only feel tolerated?

- When you consider your relationship with the Father, do you feel he treasures you or tolerates you?

- Was your family affectionate growing up? How do you think this affected you?

- Where in your story has abandonment played out? Have you ever felt burned as I did when my church asked me to leave after only four months?

- I experienced a love encounter with the Father when my friend sat on my lap and told me that God doesn't tolerate me, he treasures me. Have you had a tangible love encounter with the Father? How did that play out? If not, have you asked for a tangible love encounter with the Father?

Created – The Source of Purpose

- What do you believe your purpose is on earth? How are you living into that?
- Are you experiencing unity with God and those in his Body? If not, what is thwarting that unity?
- What is the center of your universe?
- Are you holding onto your independence?
- What would it look like to open space to let God speak?
- Do you believe God wants to use you as a channel to speak his value into others?

From Respect to Wisdom

- With which of the root sins do you most identify?
- Where do you see the desire to be respected in your life?
- What is your attitude toward failure?
- To what information do you feel entitled?
- Do you believe you are God's beloved son or daughter with whom he is well pleased?
- How are you seeking to Lord to find wisdom for others?

Jeremiah 13 – The Ruined Loincloth

- What do you feel is soiled or ruined in your story? How have you seen God start to redeem this? How do you think he'll keep redeeming it?
- Are there places of stubbornness you have with the Lord?
- What do you believe is God's destination for you?
- Are you living from the affirmations God has spoken over you?
- How has God fathered you?

From Value to Inspiration

- Do you have a deep need to be valued? How are you filling that need?
- Do you feel significant? Why or why not? What makes someone significant?
- Do anyone know your true identity?
- Has the Father shown you the value of others? Have you asked him to do so?
- How have you spoken value over others?

Philippians 2 – Entitlements and the Cross

- To what do you feel entitled? What would it look like

to lay down those entitlements?

- What are you self-protecting?
- Why are you self-protecting?
- What does it look like to follow Jesus' example of laying your life down?
- What do you do when you experience loss or the threat of loss to your respect, value, or love?

From Love to Peacemaking

- Do you fear offending someone?
- What do you fear others might disapprove of in you?
- To what comforts do you cling?
- Who's opinions of you hold more sway over your thoughts and actions, the Father's or other people's?
- What makes you anxious?
- Where have you felt abandoned?
- To what relationships do you feel entitled?
- How do you avoid discomfort?
- Where is there potential in your life for peacemaking?

The Tempter

- What tempts you?
- Jesus lifted up those who had lost their dignity. Where

do you see him doing this in your life?

- How are you speaking dignity into people who have lost it?
- Do you believe Jesus was tempted as you are?
- What would it look like to draw near to Jesus in the midst of temptation? What keeps a person from doing so?

Interacting Longings – The Interplay of Fulfillments

- When others confront you, what triggers in you?
- Picture the last emotional scene within your family or workplace. What were people's underlying needs?
- What is your first response to stress and pain?
- What would it look like to lower the emotional noise in your heart?
- How does the root sin with which you struggle manifest in your unique personality?
- What heart needs do you feel are unmet?

Genesis 3 – The Tree

- What in your life feels embarrassing, frightening, or wrong?
- Where do you hide?
- What do you hide?

- Do you experience intimacy? Where? If not, what's standing in the way of that?
- Who do you trust?
- Do you believe God has his glory and your benefit in mind?
- What emotional noise is too loud in your life?

THREE ROOT MOTIVATIONS

	Their basic desire:	When their basic desire is not met:	They are motivated to:	Others may experience them as:	Helpful alternative responses for this person:	When the alternatives are taken these people offer organizations:
PRIDE-BASED PERSON	To be respected To be right	They can often feel like a failure. They may begin feel incompetent Demand Respect	Seek clarity Push for competence Garner support and action around their ideas	Competitive Assertive/Purposeful Prideful/Arrogant Use people as resources	Move to Humility Learn how to bring people along to the vision Commit to being empathetic	Wisdom: The ability to assess needs and gaps and formulate plans quickly Leading with confidence
SELF-BASED PERSON	To be valued To be significant	They can feel worthless and believe they are unheard and misunderstood	See themselves as significant because of what they offer Seek value among those who promote them or advance their status	Political Strategic Deceptive and Vague Unpredictable Aloof Not genuine Use people for attention	Find significance and identity apart from what they have to offer Commit to being genuine Allow people to be themselves	Inspiration: They enhance the value of others by helping others see what they do well
FEAR-BASED PERSON	To be free from pain and conflict	They may feel disliked and uncared for and afraid	To be liked and loved by all Avoid pain and seek comfort Please people	Caretakers People pleasers Insecure Conflict avoiders Use people as comforters	Recognize that others opinions of them do not define them. Show prophetic courage	Peace: Knowing how to care for others and being sensitive to community needs to bring calm and stability

Made in the USA
Columbia, SC
26 June 2018